MY PLACE IN SPACE

by Robin and Sally Hirst

illustrated by
Roland Harvey with Joe Levine

ORCHARD BOOKS   NEW YORK

Orchard Books, A division of Franklin Watts, Inc. 387 Park Avenue South, New York, NY 10016

Printed by General Offset Co., Inc. Bound by Horowitz/Rae. Manufactured in the
United States of America. The text of this book is set in 16 pt. Novarese Medium.
The illustrations are pen and ink and watercolor, and airbrushed paintings.
Book design by Mina Greenstein   10 9 8 7 6 5 4 3 2

Library of Congress Cataloging-in-Publication Data
Hirst, Robin. My place in space / by Robin and Sally Hirst ; illustrated by Roland
Harvey with Joe Levine.—1st American ed.   p.   cm. Summary: Henry tells the bus
driver exactly where he lives, positioning himself precisely in the universe.
ISBN 0-531-05859-X   ISBN 0-531-08459-0 (lib. bdg.)
1. Astronomy—Juvenile literature.   [1. Astronomy.]   I. Hirst, Sally.   II. Harvey, Roland,
ill.   III. Levine, Joe, ill.   IV. Title. QB46.H57   1990   520—dc20   89-37893   CIP   AC

MY PLACE
IN SPACE

Not so long ago, Henry Wilson and his sister Rosie were waiting for a bus. When it arrived, the door swung open, and a tall, rather scruffy driver peered down from the top of the steps.

"What's your name, sonny?"
"Henry Wilson," replied Henry politely. "And this is my sister Rosie."
"And what can we do for you?" asked the driver.
"We would like to go home," said Henry.

"Home?" asked the driver rather loudly.
Henry wished the man would speak a little more softly.
"Home?" repeated the driver just as loudly. "Are you sure you know where you live?"

The bus driver laughed and winked at two young women
sitting at the front of the bus. They began to giggle.

"Do you know where you live?" asked the driver. Everyone on
the bus stared at Henry.

Henry gritted his teeth and took a deep breath.
"Yes, I do. We live at 12 Main Street, Gumbridge. Our house is
on the north side of Main Street. The town of Gumbridge is just over
the river."

Henry looked at the driver, whose grin was fading slightly. It seemed as though the man wanted to speak, but no words were coming out of his mouth. Henry took a deep breath and continued. "Gumbridge is just a typical country town in Australia.

"Australia is in the southern hemisphere of the planet Earth,"
continued Henry. The driver stopped laughing.

Rosie squeezed Henry's hand. Henry, gaining courage, took another deep breath and went on.

"The planet Earth is one of nine known planets which circle the star we call the sun. Earth is the third planet from the sun, 93 million miles away from it. In fact, it takes eight minutes for the sun's light to travel to Earth. That may seem a long way, but it's 3.7 billion miles to Pluto, the ninth planet from the sun. Sunlight takes about five and a half hours to travel to Pluto."

Rosie, who had not taken her eyes off Henry, nodded her head in agreement, but the driver said nothing, even though his jaw was moving up and down. "We call the sun and planets our solar system," continued Henry.

"The solar system is in the middle of a group of stars we call the solar neighborhood. Our sun's neighbors are stars of all colors and sizes. You can see them in the dark skies of Gumbridge on any clear night. The nearest star is called Alpha Centauri. It takes over four years for its starlight to reach Earth.

"Other stars, like the big red star Antares, are way out at the edge of the solar neighborhood, about 500 light-years away. That means it takes 500 years for their light to reach us."

Rosie smiled at Henry and took another deep breath, just like him.

"Our solar neighborhood is just a small part of the Orion Arm. That's a giant curve in space made of millions of stars gathered in solar neighborhoods. Among the stars are huge clouds of dust and glowing gases.

"You can see the dust clouds from Gumbridge, too. They look like dark patches in the very starry parts of the sky."

The driver checked his watch. He looked as though he was about to say something, but Henry quickly continued.

"The Orion Arm is just one of the arms of a huge group of about 300 billion stars. This whole group is called the Milky Way Galaxy. If you think it's a long way to Gumbridge, or even to the nearest star, that's nothing really—it takes light one hundred thousand years to cross from one side of the galaxy to the other.

"Our galaxy is called a spiral galaxy because of the way its arms make a spiral shape." Henry let go of Rosie's hand so that he could demonstrate the shape of the spiral arms.

"Of course the Milky Way isn't the only galaxy in space. There are twenty galaxies in our local group of galaxies. Ours is the second largest. The largest is called the Andromeda Galaxy. It's a spiral galaxy too," said Henry, making more spiral shapes for the driver.

"Light from the stars in the Andromeda Galaxy takes over 2 million years to reach our galaxy. Most of space is just that—space," added Henry, trying to relieve the driver's puzzled look.

The driver's face was turning slightly red. Henry went on, "Our local group of galaxies is just part of a huge group of galaxies called the Virgo Supercluster.

"It takes light a few million years to cross our local group of galaxies, but it takes a few hundred million years to cross from one side of a supercluster to another."

The driver's face was now bright red, and he was shaking his head from side to side.

Henry took one more deep breath and, waving both arms to make a large circle, he said, "And the whole universe is filled with superclusters of galaxies!"

Rosie stepped forward. Clenching her fists and standing up straight, she said, "So we do know where we live.

"We live at 12 Main Street, Gumbridge, Australia, Southern
Hemisphere . . .

. . . Earth . . .

. . . solar system . . .

... solar neighborhood ...

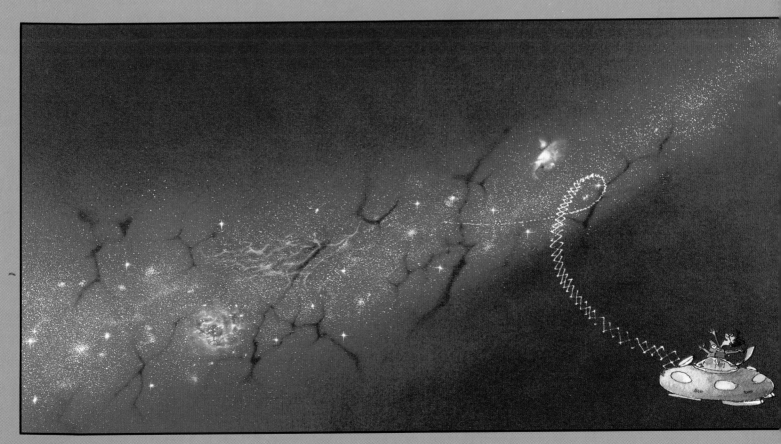

... Orion Arm ...

. . . Milky Way Galaxy . . .

. . . local group of galaxies . . .

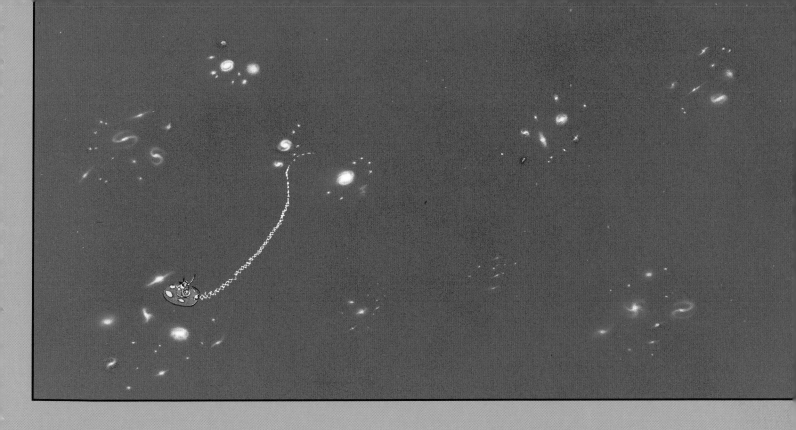

. . . Virgo Supercluster . . .

. . . the universe. . . . "

"May we get on the bus, now, please?" asked Henry.

More About Space

The pictures in this book give some idea just how big the universe is. The distances in outer space are so great that they can't be measured the same way we measure distances on Earth. From Earth to the sun alone is 93 million miles. That is 3,500 times around the earth. The nearest star, Alpha Centauri, is over 25 trillion miles away. So, if the sun were the size of a tennis ball, the earth would be the size of a grain of sand, and almost 23 feet away. Alpha Centauri would also be the size of a tennis ball, but 1,240 miles further on.

Henry knows that light travels about 186,000 miles each second. That means that light could travel around the earth seven times in one second. A light-second is the distance of 186,000 miles. Light travels the distance from Earth to the sun in 8 minutes, so that distance is called 8 light-minutes. A light-year is the distance light travels in one year. This is almost 6 trillion miles. Just think how long it would take you to travel that far by car. Our nearest galaxy, Andromeda, is over 2 million light-years away!

On a clear night you can see about two thousand stars in the sky. From a dark location, you should also be able to see the Milky Way, which appears as a whitish glow across the heavens. If you look very carefully at the brightest stars, you might notice their different colors— some are more orange, some more blue. Take a look!